MW00816691

"Wayne Grudem is one of those ve. ... ...
speaks and writes with equal clarity and faithfulness. That's why
listening is often even more satisfying than reading. I am glad his
voice (and heart) is now available in this way."

Dr. John Piper
Pastor of Bethlehem Baptist Church & prolific author

"Formal theological training was never a privilege I enjoyed. But
had I attended seminary, I would have wanted to learn theology in
Wayne Grudem's classroom. This DVD series now makes this
possible for me—and for you."

C J Mahaney
Sovereign Grace Ministries

"This is a great resource from one of the world's best theology
teachers."

Mark Driscoll
Pastor of Mars Hill Church & President of the
Acts 29 Church Planting Network

"These truly are twenty basic beliefs that every Christian should
know. Wayne Grudem is a master teacher with the ability to explain profound truths in simple language. He is a man of deep
conviction and theological passion—and those who watch these
DVDs will be both educated and encouraged in the faith."

Dr. Al Mohler
President of the Southern Baptist Theological Seminary

"This is a top quality production designed to help Christians deepen their understanding of the key truths of the Bible. Imagine having the services of a world class theologian and author available to your church for twenty weeks! Thanks to Clear Cut Media that is now a possibility for congregations large and small.

This is a resource that deserves the widest possible use."

Ian Coffey
Director of Leadership Training, Moorlands Bible College, UK

"As one of the most brilliant Bible scholars of our generation, Wayne Grudem takes the core beliefs of our faith and makes them practical for followers of Jesus Christ—new and mature alike. This is an invaluable resource—get it for your church and use it!"

Dr. James MacDonald
Senior Pastor, Harvest Bible Chapel

Wayne Grudem

CHRISTIAN BELIEFS

LIFE TRANSFORMING TRUTHS

Study Guide
by Clear Cut Media

CLEARCUTMEDIA

Published by Clear Cut Media
            250 Monroe NW, Suite 400,
            Grand Rapids, Michigan, 49503

Originally published in the UK 2009
First USA edition 2010

Printed in China

Email: info@clearcutmedia.tv
Web: www.clearcutmedia.tv/us

ISBN-13:   978-0-9557042-3-9
ISBN-10:   0-9557042-3-5

With thanks to Zondervan for granting copyright permission for Systematic Theology and Christian Beliefs.

Scripture quotations are from The Holy Bible, English Standard Version® (ESV®), copyright © 2001 by Crossway, a publishing ministry of Good News Publishers. Used by permission. All rights reserved.

10 9 8 7 6 5 4 3 2 1

Table of Contents

Introduction 3

1. What is the Bible? 6

2. What is God like? 12

3. What is the Trinity? 20

4. What is creation? 28

5. What is prayer? 35

6. What are angels and demons? 42

7. What is man? 48

8. What is sin? 54

9. Who is Christ? 62

10. What is atonement? 71

11. What is the resurrection? 80

12. What is election (or predestination)? 88

13. What does it mean to become a Christian? 98

14. What are justification and adoption? 107

15. What are sanctification and perseverance? 118

16. What is death? 126

17. What is the church? 136

18. What will happen when Christ returns? 147

19. What is the final judgment? 155

20. What is heaven? 165

Introduction

"May grace and peace be multiplied to you
in the knowledge of God and of Jesus our Lord"
(2 Peter 1:2)

This study guide and DVD course will provide you with a solid grounding in the foundations of the Christian faith. The study guide and DVD are based on the introductory book, *Christian Beliefs* by Wayne Grudem, edited by Elliot Grudem, which you may wish to read in conjunction with the DVD. For more detailed discussions of these topics, see the medium-length *Bible Doctrine* by Wayne Grudem, edited by Jeff Purswell or the larger book *Systematic Theology* by Wayne Grudem.

How to use this study guide

This study guide, produced by Clear Cut Media, is designed to be used in conjunction with the DVD series in a number of different formats ranging from larger group settings to smaller home Bible study groups and individual discipleship programs. Each DVD session lasts approximately 40 minutes and has optional discussion breaks, with discussion questions in this study guide. A 'going deeper' section is provided in this study guide for those wanting extended discussion. In conjunction with the Q&A sections, 'going deeper' will help you build on what you have learned using the three great principles for discipleship taken from Ezra 7:10, "For Ezra had set his heart **to study** the Law of the Lord, and **to do** it and **to teach** his statutes and rules in Israel."

- → Know it
- → Do it
- → Teach it

A leader's guide with helpful answers and suggestions for group work can be downloaded at www.clearcutmedia.tv/us.

Additional Resources

The following resources related to the *Christian Beliefs* course can be purchased on the Clear Cut Media website, along with other resources selected for their unusual quality and usefulness in helping Christians grow.

- Leader's Guide
  A full leader's guide can be purchased as a download. The leader's guide provides information on using this curriculum, along with discussion aids and answers to the questions in the study guides. An invaluable resource for anyone leading a small group.

- Video Downloads
  All sessions are available as video downloads from the Clear Cut Media website. Ideal if you are in a small group and have missed a session or want to re-enforce your learning.

- Study Guide
  Additional Study guides can be purchased on the Clear Cut Media website.

- *Christian Beliefs* Book
  Christian Beliefs: Twenty Basics Every Christian Should Know by Wayne Grudem, edited by Elliot Grudem. This book is the basis for the DVD course and a great additional study aid.

- *Systematic Theology* Book
  An Introduction to Biblical Doctrine by Wayne Grudem. Purchase this volume for a more detailed and comprehensive discussion of the Christian Beliefs course.

www.clearcutmedia.tv/us

Key to the Study Guide

To help you navigate and get the most out of this Study Guide each chapter is divided into four sections. The pictures below introduce each section.

INTRODUCTION which highlights the main teaching points for the session.

SUMMARY of the session which will help you get a 'big picture' view of the session and where you will be going.

QUESTIONS which relate to the discussion breaks on the DVD.

GOING DEEPER section which offers you the option to be able to take the material deeper, advance your study and apply it to your life.

What is the Bible?

Introduction

Through the words of the Bible itself, we are told of God's view of the world, how we should live, what we should do and what God thinks of the Bible itself.

"But is it the truth?"

In this session, the authority, clarity, necessity and sufficiency of the Bible will be discussed, expounded and built upon.

We will be led from the Old Testament through to the New Testament in the context of the people who wrote the Bible, with each section personally applied, encouraging us to live our lives the way God wants.

"Should we believe everything that we read in the Bible?"

Summary

Authority

From the Old Testament to the New, the words of the Bible are the words of God. In the Old Testament, these words were given in many forms such as directly from God (the Ten Commandments), as a record of what people actually did and as records of dreams and hymns of praise.

God, through Jesus, also gave the Apostles the authority to write and authorize additional words for the Bible forming the New Testament.

We will be led to think about why we believe this is the Word of God—that we must be guided by the Spirit to understand the truth, though external evidence does have some value.

We will then see that there are no contradictions or mistakes in the Bible and that the Bible has not been corrupted over the years.

Questions

The words in the Bible are the words of God. How do we know God was involved in their writing when they were physically written by human authors?

Do you think the Bible is the authoritative Word of God? Why is that?

Have you ever thought about possible contradictions and mistakes in the Bible? What are they, and have they worried you? How can you handle these?

Clarity

Some of the Bible is hard to understand, and some is easy. However, God caused the Bible to be written in a way everyone could understand. Any disagreements over meaning are caused by the readers themselves, not by the actual words of God.

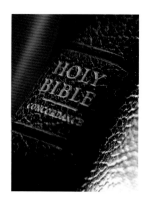

We are shown a method to deal with difficult passages:

- Pray for help to understand—God wants us to!

- Study with others and with useful books.

However, as we grow as Christians, we find that much of the Bible is actually not that hard to understand, and we increasingly understand it.

Questions

It is tempting to skip the difficult passages of the Bible. Why should we try to understand more by studying these passages?

Do you find the Bible difficult to understand? What methods can you use to understand more of it?

Necessity

One of the most asked questions in the Christian life is, "how can I know God's will?" The Bible helps us with this through:

- Knowing the way of salvation

- Knowing God personally

- Knowing with certainty what God wants us to do

- Helping us to serve God better

It gives us a sure knowledge of God's will, and there is no other certain source to discover this will.

Questions

Can you think of any examples of how the Bible shows us how to live today?

We may say the Bible is necessary for our lives, but in what ways do we actually apply its teaching in everyday life?

Why is it necessary to apply the Bible's teaching?

Sufficiency

Differing faiths and religions, such as Judaism and Mormonism, believe you can know God through means other than the Bible, such as the teachings of organizations, other holy books and leaders.

However, since the Bible is the Word of God, it is sufficient for us to know what He wants us to do. Even the Bible itself tells us that the words contained within it are sufficient for us to "walk in the law of the LORD" (Psalm 119:1).

We cannot, and do not need to, add to the teachings of Scripture to live the Christian life—it is sufficient for every good work (2 Timothy 3:16–17).

Questions

Do we sometimes take sources other than the Bible as God's truth? If so, what are some examples of the sources and how we might use them?

The New Testament was written two thousand years ago. Is it sufficient for, and relevant to, our 'modern' lives? Why?

How would you answer someone who asked why you based your life on the Bible?

Going Deeper

Know it:

→ Watch the Q&A session and discuss in depth.

Do it:

→ Take a difficult passage of Scripture and work through the process of understanding it.

Teach it:

→ Explain to at least one other person this week why you believe the Bible is the Word of God.

2 What is God Like?

Introduction

The Bible tells us that we are created in God's image and that we were created for His honor and praise. Yet we often do not stop to actually think about what God is like.

"What is God actually like?"

In this session, some of the attributes of God will be discussed. We will be shown how they can affect the way we live our lives, both now and in the future.

In our lives, we should seek to be more like God, and do our best to acquire His qualities and attributes. By knowing more of what God is like, we can learn increasingly to appreciate, trust and adore Him.

"Are you living your life exhibiting the qualities and attributes of God?"

Summary

Attributes of God—Part 1

The Bible tells us that God exists, and that even 'non-believers' know of His existence (Romans 1:21). Just as a wrist watch is not created by chance, God's creation did not happen by chance.

God wants us to know Him personally. He created us in His own image. Every leaf on every tree calls out to us saying, "God made *me*," and almost everyone calls out to God when they are in a crisis. Creation is a witness to an infinitely powerful God.

The nature of God is revealed to man through the words of the Bible. We are shown that God is INDEPENDENT of mankind. He does not need us for His existence, but He is glad and sings with joy about us. We too should have joy. He did not need to create us, but He did it anyway!

God is eternally UNCHANGEABLE. He acts differently in different situations according to our responses to Him, but the core of God is never changing. This means we can trust Him to be just and fair.

God is ETERNAL. He existed before the world began and will be with us throughout eternity. We ourselves exist in time, so we should learn to use our time for God's glory.

God is OMNIPRESENT. He is present in every part of space and time. We can use this knowledge to take away our fear of going anywhere in obedience to God. But we should also remember that we cannot flee from Him.

Questions

Do you think some of the attributes of God are visible in our lives? Which ones?

Sometimes we are not happy, even though we may be successful. How could a knowledge of God's attributes help us to be more fulfilled?

In which situations of our daily lives could we actively choose to be more like God?

Attributes of God—Part 2

God is SPIRIT. This means He has no physical body, size or dimension. However, He brought the whole universe into existence and is infinitely powerful. We should learn that God does not want to be represented as any created thing.

God is OMNISCIENT. He knows everything including the past, the present and the future in every detail. Understanding this helps us to know that nothing will ever surprise God. He always knows what is best for us.

God is WISE. He has chosen the best goals and the best ways to achieve them. He also wants us to grow in wisdom. We should enjoy learning because it makes us more like God.

God is TRUTHFUL. He only speaks the truth, and we should do the same.

God is LOVE. We could have a God who did not care for us. That would be terrible, but thankfully we see that our God is continually loving to us. Just as God loves us, we are commanded to love our neighbor as we love ourselves.

Questions

How does knowing the attributes of God help us to trust Him and worship Him more deeply?

Mankind has often tried to represent God using symbols and idols. What are your thoughts about these? Does God want us to 'create' an image of Him?

Is there some reflection of God in your life? How can you make it stronger?

Attributes of God—Part 3

God is HOLY. This means that He is separated from all evil and sin. To be more like God, we too should not participate in evil things. Instead we should seek God's honor.

God is RIGHTEOUS AND JUST. He always does what is right and acts in accordance with what is right. This means God must punish sin. God has guaranteed that all accounts will be settled on the Day of Judgment.

God is JEALOUS. He continually seeks to protect His own honor, and He desires that worship is given only to Him. In the same way that we do not like it when people lie about us, God only wants the truth told about Himself.

God is BLESSED. He takes delight in all things that reflect His character. This means that as we grow to reflect His attributes, we too will grow in joy.

Finally, God is INFINITE. He is a most wonderful and excellent being who is not subject to any of the limitations of humanity, and yet we are made in His image.

Questions

Is there ever a danger of emphasizing one of God's attributes over the others?

Now that you know more about God's nature, how could this assist to deepen your prayer life?

Is there a difference between knowing about God and knowing God?

Going Deeper

Know it:

→ Watch the question on open theism and discuss both its implications and Biblical answers.

Do it:

→ Have a time of prayer in which you recount the wonders of God and praise Him for who He is.

Teach it:

→ Pick two of the attributes of God and write a summary of them along with the pastoral implications. Give your summary to at least three people this week for their encouragement.

3 What is the Trinity?

Introduction

In church life, we often refer to God as being our Father. We discuss and learn about Jesus, and we ask the Holy Spirit to fill us and work through us. Yet we only have one God.

"How can this be?"

In this session, we learn about the doctrine of the Trinity—one God in three persons. The difficulties that arise when we consider the nature of God are numerous, yet it is essential that we understand what and who God actually is.

So, just who is God, and how do we understand more about Him?

Summary

The Doctrine of Trinity

The word 'Trinity' is not actually mentioned in the Bible, but the Bible often mentions the different persons of God.

- God is three persons. When Jesus was baptized, the Spirit descended from heaven as a dove, and the voice of God was heard—all three persons of God acted at the same time, but in different ways (Matthew 3:13–17).

- Each person is fully God. Few question that God is the Father. The Bible tells us that the Son is also God. Jesus also told us that the Holy Spirit was God. He told us to baptize in the name of the Father, Son and Holy Spirit (Matthew 28:19).

- There is only one God. The Bible says this in many places (Deuteronomy 6:4).

How can this be?

The Bible encourages us to use our logic to understand things, but does not ask us to believe in a contradiction. The doctrine of Trinity is not a contradiction; it is just a mystery.

Christian Beliefs Study Guide

Questions

When you think deeply about how there can be one God as three persons, it is hard to understand. How have you tried to understand it, or had it explained to you?

God is all three persons—which person of the Trinity have you most focused on and why?

Why do non-Christians have a difficult time accepting this doctrine?

Using analogies to describe God

It is tempting to try to understand the doctrine of the Trinity by comparing God to things in His creation, or to other things that we can comprehend:

- A tree—roots, trunk and branches
- Water—ice, water and steam
- A pie—split into three sections
- A pie (Father) with extra sections (Jesus and the Holy Spirit)
- One person acting in three different ways

But *none* of these truly explain the Biblical truth of one God in three persons. God has told us that He has kept some knowledge to Himself (Deuteronomy 29:29).

It can help us to think of God as a complete circle, with all of the circle being the Father, all of the circle being the Son and all of the circle being the Spirit; yet the Father, Son and Spirit are distinct persons! This is the mystery of the Trinity.

Questions

We are told that the Jehovah's Witnesses claim that Jesus and the Holy Spirit were created by God the Father. How does this go against what the Scriptures say?

Have you heard someone say that they "have it all figured out?" What would you now say to someone who claims to understand the Trinity?

Does it matter to you that God is three-in-one, each fully God? How can this affect the way we pray and praise God?

The different roles of the Trinity

Each person of the Trinity existed before creation and each is completely God. Yet each member of the Trinity has a different role and there seems to be an order of authority.

- God the Father directs, plans and commands. He has the ultimate authority.

- God the Son (Jesus) is obedient and sits at the right hand of God.

- God the Spirit was sent into the world by the Father and the Son.

Marriage, the workplace and churches are earthly representations of this difference in authority, with each member being an equal, with their own roles and yet an essential part of the whole.

God's wisdom is shown when people from different backgrounds come together as one church and are united in His name. Paul said, "For just as the body is one and has many members, and all the members of the body, though many, are one body, so it is with Christ" (1 Corinthians 12:12).

The mystery of the Trinity should leave us in awe of who God is and should evoke reverence and worship.

There is an order of authority, and yet all members of the Trinity are completely God.

Questions

What difficulties do you have in understanding the doctrine of the Trinity? Can you live with the mystery now?

Mankind naturally seeks to put one person in power. Examples include presidents, kings, politicians and priests. What is right and what can be wrong about this? Does it reflect how our God wants us to act in authority relationships?

In our relationships, marriages and work place, should we feel happier knowing that even Jesus was submissive and obedient to another?

Going Deeper

Know it:

↪ Watch Q&A and discuss.

↪ Demonstrate from Scripture that the Holy Spirit is a person and not an 'it'.

Do it:

↪ Write a brief article on why the deity of Christ is important for salvation.

Teach it:

↪ Explain to another Christian why cults do not accept the doctrine of the Trinity and why Christians do.

4 What is creation?

Introduction

Where did the universe come from? Has it always existed? Is it good or evil?

The Bible tells us that God created everything in the universe by His Word (Psalm 33:6).

Scientists try to explain creation in a variety of ways, such as the 'Big Bang' theory (without God). They explain the diversity of life with various theories of evolution. Scientific theories seem to explain a lot of things, and although some parts are in agreement with the Bible, others are not.

Then there is the question of whether God interacts with His creation. Is He in everything we see? Is He there, but uncaring? Is there a war between good and evil? Maybe there is no God at all?

"Does all this matter at all?"
"Did God create the universe?"

Summary

Biblical creation or human theories?

In Genesis 1 we are told that God created the universe, starting with the light of day. Then He created the heavens above, the earth, plants, stars and animals. Finally, He created man and woman who were made in His own likeness. Only humans are made in His likeness; not even angels bear this similarity!

Some secular scientists support the Big Bang theory, which pre-supposes the existence of matter and energy. Biblical creation's teaching says that God created the universe out of nothing! There is also the theory of macro-evolution, that life is created from random mutations with no purpose from God. This does not give us the dignity of created beings that the study of Biblical creation gives us.

For many years, 'Science' has been pitted against 'Biblical Creation Theories', but it is important to accept that God created science, and that they are not opposed to each other *per se*. A Biblical view of creation is only opposed to some elements of secular science which challenge the facts of the Bible.

God is pro-science! After all, God knows all scientific fact and the universe was created for God's purpose, to give Him glory!

Questions

What are your thoughts on creation, as described at the beginning of Genesis?

The theories of the Big Bang and evolution are widely accepted. Do you accept them too? How do they fit into the Biblical creation story?

There are many scientific discoveries at the moment which seem to involve mankind 'playing' with creation. What are your thoughts on genetic science?

Other views of God and creation

Materialism—Matter + Time + Chance, without any help from God. A materialist does not pray because it is believed there is no one to whom to pray. Much of modern culture comes from this point of view.

Deism—There is a God who creates but does not intervene with the ongoing functionality of creation. A deist does not pray because his God does not care. Instead, this God lets things run on their own.

Dualism—God and the universe have always existed, and Good and Evil also have always existed. This is the "Star Wars" theory of life seen in many Eastern religions. With this view which side should you pray to?

Pantheism—God is in everything that we see and is not separate from the universe. This is seen in Eastern and tribal religions where people worship animals or objects. You can pray to anything you want, but who knows if there will be an answer?

We must be careful not to let these other views of God and creation enter our thinking. Christianity and Judaism are the only religions who have an infinite God separate from creation and also involved in it. God is actually involved with us.

Questions

How well do we hold together the truths that God is both transcendent and personal?

Why are so many people drawn to other views of creation and God?

In our daily lives, how can we help others to see God as separate from and also involved in the universe?

The purpose of creation

The purpose of creation is to give glory to God. If we look, we see reflections of Him in everything. He wants us to discover it and thank Him for it. God made everything and then said that it was good.

We should also delight in things made from the earth, such as houses and computers. Everything should fill us with delight. When we invent and discover things, we are imitating the wisdom and creativity of our Creator.

We should not misuse nature or waste it, but rule over it and subdue it as God intended. The ideal in God's eyes is not an untouched nature, but a wisely used nature glorifying God.

Questions

Environmental issues are hot news at the moment. How can we hold a healthy respect for technological advance with good stewardship of the earth's resources?

Describe your experiences of awe at God's creation.

Going Deeper

Know it:

- → Watch the Q&A and discuss.
- → How would you help someone who felt the Bible was not consistent with science?

Do it:

- → This week as you go about your daily life, focus sharply on the creation around you and practice praising God for what you see and what it tells you about Him.

Teach it:

- → Practice taking people from creation to the cross in your conversations this week.

What is prayer?

Introduction

Prayer is a personal communication with God in which we can confess our sins, worship and praise Him, and make requests. Through prayer, we can actually affect what happens and influence history itself.

The Bible has many examples of prayers being answered, but it also has examples of prayers not being answered. Often our failure to receive is because we never asked in the first place. We don't have because we don't ask. The Bible tells us that what we ask for in faith will be given to us (John 14:13–14).

- Does God hear the prayers of unbelievers?
- What does it mean to pray in Jesus' name?
- What is praying according to God's will?
- What can hinder our prayers?
- And what about our own unanswered prayers?

"In seeking to understand prayer, we are in good company."

Summary

All who ask shall receive

Although God knows what we need before we ask Him, He set up the world so that we could ask for things over a period of time to increase our dependence on Him.

Prayer:

- Is a personal communication with God
- Deepens our relationship with Him
- Allows us to influence history

God has allowed us to be involved with world events and, if we ask according to His will, we will receive real-time answers! Scripture shows that we can actually impact eternity through our prayers.

However, we only have the right to ask God because Jesus has cleansed us from our sins. Unbelievers do not have the right of access to God, but He sometimes answers their prayers out of His mercy.

Praying in Jesus' name does not mean we have to say "in the name of Jesus, Amen." It means we should pray in a way that is consistent with Jesus' qualities and His authority.

Questions

What we pray for can actually change history. How should this affect our prayer lives?

God knows what we need, so why should we bother praying? And why should we pray over a period of time?

What are your experiences of prayer?

Prayer according to God's will

When we pray, we must submit ourselves to God's will because He knows what is best for us. This means that there are *two* classes of prayer:

- Those things which the Bible tells us are God's Will.

- Those things which are not mentioned in the Bible.

If something is in the Bible, we do not need to ask "if this is what you want, then..." in our prayers. But if we do not know what God's will is on a subject, it is better to state the facts as we see them in our prayers, and then wait and listen for God.

Jesus, in Mark 11:24, encourages us to pray believing that we have already received the answer. However, this does not mean that we need to affirm our prayers loudly over and over. God encourages faith-filled prayer, having a "conviction of things not seen" (Hebrews 11:1) and trusting that, "Shall not the Judge of all the earth do what is just?" (Genesis 18:25).

As we grow in our knowledge of God and His will, our prayers will become more effective, as we remember that sin hinders the effectiveness of our prayer life (Psalm 66:18).

Isn't it inspiring to think that the God of the universe actually listens to us as we pray?

Questions

Ask and you will receive. Give examples of appropriate and inappropriate prayer requests.

What things should we pray about regularly?

How can we listen to God more effectively?

What if prayers seem unanswered?

"God opposes the proud, but gives grace to the humble" (James 4:6).

We may pray righteously, but sometimes our prayers are still seemingly not answered. Even then God never leaves us or forsakes us (Hebrews 13:5).

When prayer is not answered the way we would like, we are in great company. Paul prayed repeatedly for the "thorn in His flesh" to be removed, but it was not (2 Corinthians 12:7–9). Therefore, we must still trust in God.

We should consider that sometimes "No" is the answer that is best for us! Even if prayer is not always answered immediately, God still invites us to pray and speak to Him. He hears us and answers our prayers, in His time, for His glory.

Questions

Jesus tells us to persevere in prayer. What does this mean in everyday life?

What can hinder our prayers? How can we overcome these problems?

Take some time now to come to God with faith-filled prayer.

Going Deeper

Know it:

→ Watch the Q&A and discuss.

→ Have a look at some of the prayers in Paul's letters and make a list of the things he prays for.

Do it:

→ Choose one or two people and focus on praying for them this week based on the list you made. Why not start a prayer journal?

→ Think about the amount of time you currently spend each day in prayer and consider how you may need to re-structure and re-prioritize your day.

Teach it:

→ Go to the people you are praying for and explain to them that you are praying the things on your list for them. If it seems appropriate, ask them if you could pray with them now.

6 What are angels and demons?

Introduction

The Bible tells us of the existence of spiritual beings, of angels. It tells us God created these beings and that they are occasionally even visible to people. He uses angels to do His work in our world as ministering spirits to support us.

The Bible also tells us of demons and of their leader, Satan himself. It tells us that demons are fallen angels who have disobeyed God. Their aim is to use any way possible to distract us from the way of Christ.

"But what do angels and demons actually do, and what powers do they really have?"

Summary

Angels

Angels were created by God to serve Him. The Bible tells us there is a 'host', or an angelic army, who carry out God's commands. They are ministering spirits who can take on human shape and form. We do not normally see them, but if God  opens our eyes it is possible to see them, just as they were seen in Biblical times.

The purpose of angels is to guard and protect Christians and to do God's will. They have great power according to the will of God. They have high intelligence and, when first created, they could choose to sin. Some angels in fact did choose to sin, and God did not spare them.

Angels also serve as examples of how to obey God. They continuously worship and glorify Him. When we come into the presence of God in worship, there are angels there worshipping with us.

However, we must not pray *to* or worship angels themselves since they are only servants of God, not God Himself. More than this, we must not accept distorted, false Gospels from 'angels'. Only the Gospel of Christ as seen in the Bible is the true Gospel.

Questions

What are your thoughts about having invisible angels to guard and protect you?

What characteristics of angels should we imitate to help us worship God more effectively?

If God is everywhere and all powerful, why do you think He created angels to help with His work?

Demons

Demons are evil angels who have sinned against God and now work evil in the world. They did not start out as evil, but they rebelled and disobeyed God. God did not spare them, and cast them out of His presence.

The leader of the demons is given many names in the Bible, such as Satan, the Devil, the Serpent, Beelzebub, the Ruler of this World, the Prince of the Power of the Air and the Evil One. We are told in the Bible that Satan was a murderer and is the father of all lies (John 8:44).

Satan tempted Jesus for forty days while He was in the desert, but Jesus overcame those temptations. Jesus also said, "Be gone, Satan" (Matthew 4:10). Satan will use any tactic possible to distract us from Christ. He uses temptation, doubt, lies, murder, false accusation, fear, confusion, sickness, envy, pride and slander.

We should be cautious and careful, but Jesus' authority and power is greater than that of Satan and his demons, so we need not be afraid. Satan and demons cannot read our minds and they cannot tell the future. Only God can do that. We are only being tricked by mystics and fortune tellers if they say otherwise. However, demons are definitely at work in the world today, so it is an error to ignore them.

We are urged to be careful and give no opportunity to the devil because he does not 'play fair'. Be careful what you write in emails; be careful about unguarded harsh comments or demeaning humor. Do not put yourself in positions where you may be tempted or where others could lie about you.

Above all, remember that Jesus triumphed over demons, and one day He will come and completely remove their power from the world.

Just as angels are an encouragement to us, demons serve as a warning to us.

Questions

How much power do you think Satan and the demons hold over mankind?

What actions can we take to remove any opportunities the devil may take advantage of in our lives?

In the Bible, both Jesus and the disciples told demons to leave people, and they left. How does James 4:7 help us in this matter?

Going Deeper

Know it:

→ Watch the Q&A and discuss.

→ How much can we say about the origin of evil?

Do it:

→ Reflect on how much attention you give to angels and demons in your everyday life. Is it balanced?

Teach it:

→ Summarize the main points you have learned this week and teach them to someone else.

What is man?

Introduction

God was not lonely before creation; He didn't need to create man. And yet He did create us and made us in His own image with many of His qualities for His glory!

For a while, God and His creation were in harmony; however, Adam and Eve sinned and were thrown out of the Garden of Eden to look after themselves. But God had a plan to save us so we could once again worship and praise Him. We represent Him here on earth and must take care of His creation.

In the first part of this session, we will learn the reasons God created man and how, in God's eyes, we are very different from the animals. We will learn that by using our creativity and knowledge we are honoring God. We will also see that sin dishonors God.

In the second part of the session, we will learn how being created in God's image matters in practical ways, and that nature is not perfect without the presence of man.

"How should being made in God's image affect our lives?"

Summary

Created in God's image

Genesis 1:27 says, "So God created man in his own image, in the image of God he created him; male and female he created them." Although God was not lonely and had no deficiency before creation, He made everything in the universe and then made man. His purpose was that we should honor Him and please Him.

Being made "in His image" means that we represent God in many ways. We know the difference between right and wrong. We have a spiritual, as well as a physical, existence. We have our amazing creativity and an ability to learn many complex languages. God takes pleasure from our becoming more like Him.

But since the very first man, Adam, people have sinned. Sin makes us less like God. If we murder, we are killing a likeness of God. Even lying causes us to be less like God.

God's purpose is that we become more and more like Christ. At the end of time, we will become fully like Jesus Christ, the Son of God, if we are born again.

Questions

Can you think of ways in which we represent the image of God?

Modern society is very concerned with 'political correctness'. What are your views on the leadership role of a man in the family? How does this relate to being made in God's image?

When we speak the truth, we become more like God. How much do the so-called 'little things' like white lies matter?

The practicalities of being created in 'God's image'

There are two main reasons being created in God's image is important in practical ways:

- We have responsibility as bearers of His image to be His representatives on earth.

- We have stewardship of His creation. We must take care of it and make it useful for our purposes.

When we sin, we represent our Creator wrongly. The earth itself was affected by the fall and by Adam's sin. But nature is not perfect by itself. God gave us the responsibility to protect and improve the earth. God has given us the unique ability to triumph over nature, but we also have the responsibility not to spoil it for future generations.

God commanded Adam and Eve to "Be fruitful and multiply" (Genesis 1:28). We should aim to fill the earth with 'God-glorifying people'. This is the purpose of Christians having children and the purpose of spreading the Gospel.

In practical ways, we should take the opportunity to make wonderful and useful things from the resources of the earth. We should delight in man's creations because our creativity is pleasing to God.

Because all human beings are created in God's image, we must have respect for people from every background, culture and race. Everyone is worthy of respect, honor and protection, including the aged, children and the unborn.

Questions

Two of the main practical points which flow from this doctrine are responsibility and stewardship. How are people today neglecting or fulfilling these responsibilities?

There is such poverty in many places around the world. Is this what God wants for human beings? How can we glorify God in this area?

Do you delight in different parts of God's creation? How can we learn to receive even more joy from them?

God commanded us to "be fruitful and multiply" and we should protect the unborn child as it is made in God's image. What are your thoughts about abortion and euthanasia? What can we do about these things?

Going Deeper

Know it:

→ Watch the Q&A and discuss.

→ What is the Bible's response to feminism? (You may wish to refer to *Evangelical Feminism and Biblical Truth* by Wayne Grudem.)

Do it:

→ This week, think of someone you might normally disdain and practice valuing them. How will you act differently?

Teach it:

→ Tell someone this week why all men and women are of equal value and the implications of this equality.

8 What is sin?

Introduction

All is not right In our families, relationships, communities and nations. Most people don't know what the ultimate cause of this is, but the Bible tells us that the cause is sin.

In this session we will learn what sin actually is, where it came from and how it affects us. We learn that right and wrong do not change and are not ultimately defined by a culture or historical period.

We don't have to teach children how to do wrong—it is just in their nature, as it is in ours. Sin affects every part of our being and the penalty for sin is death.

"So, what is sin, where did it come from, and what can we do about it?"

Summary

What is sin?

The definition of sin is "any failure to conform to the moral law of God, in act, attitude or nature."

Sinful acts include breaking the Ten Commandments, but we must remember that God wants conformity in our hearts as well as in our actions. It is not enough not to steal; we must also not have a *desire* to steal.

The world judges right and wrong in comparison to everyone else; it is measured by what everyone else is doing. But God's standard is absolute, not relative; it is moral perfection.

God created His laws in agreement with His own character. This means right and wrong are not defined by our culture or time in history, but are unchanging in all cultures for all time. We should rejoice in these unchanging moral standards.

Questions

Read Matthew 5:21–33. Personalize and discuss the practical out-workings of the sinful heart attitudes Jesus talks about in this passage.

Do you think there is a scale of sin with some worse than others?

Are the laws of our country in agreement with God's own character or based upon a 'comparison to everyone else?' Give examples.

Where did sin come from?

Biblically, God is never blamed for sin; humans are always accountable for it. God is righteous and cannot sin or do wrong. He does not tempt anyone to sin. Yet the emergence of sin in the world did not surprise God as He is omniscient. There is a mystery here—God cannot be blamed for sin, yet He created us with the capacity to sin.

Before Adam and Eve sinned, there had been sin in the angelic realm. Now, because of the fall, from the moment we are born we have a sinful nature. If we had been in the same situation as Adam and Eve, we would have made the same sinful life decision to disobey God.

With Adam, one man represented us all and brought sin to us all. This sets the stage for Jesus, whose obedience has made all Christians righteous. Our own deeds are not enough to gain any merit with God, but all who are found in Jesus are counted as righteous because He represented us (Romans 5:12–21).

Questions

God cannot sin, and yet He created Adam and Eve with the freedom to be able to sin. What are your thoughts on this mystery?

Should we blame Adam for the sin in the world, or should we be glad that we can now be represented to God through Jesus? Compare both men.

We are told that our own deeds are not enough to gain any merit with God. Therefore, should we even try to sin less? Why? What difference will it make?

How does sin affect us?

The Bible is clear that everyone, other than Jesus, sins. From the first sin, God said that the penalty for sin is death. This penalty is worked out progressively in our lives as we grow older, age, become weak and then die. But now, in Christ for all who believe, our sins are forgiven.

If we sin as Christians, our legal standing before God is not changed. We are still justified, and we will not be condemned to hell. But if we sin, we come under God's 'Fatherly displeasure'. We are still a member of His family, but He is not pleased with us

at that time. This interrupts our fellowship with Him.

God is both our Judge and our Father. Thus we should not take sin lightly as we don't want to grieve Him and lose His blessing on our lives.

To make our relationship right with God, we must pray and ask for forgiveness for our sins. This will cleanse us. But there is a warning—if a person who claims to be a Christian persists in greater and greater sin, this brings into question whether that person is truly a Christian. No one born of Christ makes a practice of sinning (1 John 3:4–6).

Questions

How is God's love for us similar to a parent's love for their children? How can this help us maintain a right relationship with God?

What effects have you seen or experienced of God's 'Fatherly displeasure' on your life? Is it worth sinning?

What should we do if we know someone who claims to be a Christian but persists in sinning? How can we help someone like this?

Going Deeper

Know it:

- → Watch the Q&A and discuss.
- → Why do you think God allows sin in the world?
- → What effect do you think sin has on a person's 'free will'?

Do it:

- → Ask the Lord to show you where you have gone soft on sin in your own life. What is your plan to correct this?

Teach it:

- → Write a summary of what you have learned from this session. Give it to a non-Christian friend to read and ask for his or her thoughts.

9 Who is Christ?

Introduction

The Bible tells us that Jesus Christ is fully man and fully God. There has never been anyone else like Him and there never will be. Jesus changed the course of history forever.

Jesus was born of a human mother through the power of the Holy Spirit. He went through childhood, learning just like other children. He worked as a carpenter for many years, and in the last three years of His life, had a ministry showing the glory of God.

He was tempted in every way, but did not sin. Yet initially, even His own brothers did not believe He was the Son of God. Finally, He died and rose again with a physical body, before ascending to heaven.

"So, who was this man called Jesus?"

Summary

Fully man

Jesus was born of a human mother, through a virgin birth by the power of the Holy Spirit. He was truly a descendant of Mary. As a child, He grew and became strong, learned to walk and run, increased in wisdom and grew in stature and in favor with God and man.

During Jesus' lifetime, He experienced human weaknesses such as hunger and tiredness and was likely to have caught illnesses just like us. He felt the whole range of human emotions, except for sinful emotions. We are told He felt joy, amazement, sadness and pain, but He did not experience covetousness, jealousy, bitterness or a fear reflecting lack of trust in God.

It is important that Jesus is fully man so He can represent us fully. Only a fully human man could die in our place. His sacrifice was better than those in the Old Testament. He is also able to sympathize fully with us because He has experienced all of life, including suffering and temptation:

- The death of a parent (Joseph probably died before Jesus was 30 years old)
- Working as a small businessman
- Physical suffering
- Betrayal
- Being lied about
- Being treated wrongly
- Being criticized, even by His own brothers

Jesus' humanity is necessary to represent us, to be a substitute for us, to die for us, to be a mediator between God and man and to be a high priest who sympathizes with our weaknesses.

Questions

Can you think of examples in which Jesus showed the same human emotions we experience?

Jesus suffered in the same ways we do. How does this help us to cope with our own problems and difficulties?

When Jesus was resurrected, He came back with a physical body. Why do you think this was important?

"Not even His brothers believed in Him" (John 7:5). What do you think it would have been like to live with Jesus as He grew up?

Fully God

As well as being fully man, the Bible makes it clear that Jesus was fully God.

Jesus Himself made the shocking statement, "before Abraham was, I am" (John 8:58). This indicates that He has existed forever, since before creation.

At the start of the book of Revelation, God is referred to as the Alpha and Omega (Revelation 1:8). At the end of the book, Jesus says that *He* is the Alpha and Omega (Revelation 22:13). This implies that God and Jesus are one and the same.

But does it matter? Jesus being fully God is important because if He were not God, we could not worship Him or pray to Him. Also, He would not have been able or qualified to bear the wrath of God for our sins.

Questions

Hebrews 1:3 says Jesus "is the radiance of the glory of God and the exact imprint of his nature." How does this show us that Jesus is fully God?

In which ways do you think Jesus has to be fully God to be able to save us?

Hebrews 1:6 says about the first born, "Let all God's angels worship him." How does this point to Christ's deity?

One person

How can it be that Jesus is both fully God and fully man? The early church came up with a number of unsatisfactory explanations before they properly answered the mystery.

- Apollonarianism—This theory taught that Jesus had a *human* body, but no human mind or spirit; rather, His *spirit* and *mind* were divine. However, this is not satisfactory because our minds and spirits, as well as our bodies, need representing and saving by Christ.

- Nestorianism—This theory insists that there really are two persons existing physically in the same body, a bit like a pantomime horse. But Jesus never spoke of Himself in this manner. He always said, "I," never, "we."

- Eutychianism—Human and divine natures join together in this theory as a third kind of being which is greater than man, but less than a deity. This theory implies that Jesus is neither God nor man and so is not a satisfactory explanation.

In the Council of Chalcedon in AD451, the church leaders and teachers agreed that the properties of each nature (man and God) were completely preserved in the one person of Christ.

This means we can have some faint analogies and some understanding, but ultimately we just have to accept by faith that Jesus was fully God and fully man and that He is more wonderful than anyone who ever lived.

Questions

Some of the greatest minds on earth have contemplated the mystery of Jesus' nature. Why is it so hard to understand that God and Jesus are one person?

Is it OK to just accept the mysteries of God by faith, or are we right to analyze and try to understand everything? Why is that?

What effect should the doctrine of Christ have on us?

Going Deeper

Know it:

- → Watch the Q&A and discuss.
- → Locate and memorize Scriptures that that teach the deity of Christ.

Do it:

- → Spend time in worship and prayer thanking God for the incarnation and its impact on your life and world history.

Teach it:

- → From memory, take someone through the Scriptures that teach the deity of Christ.

What is atonement?

Introduction

Before Jesus was born, an angel came to Joseph and told him to name this baby Jesus because, "he will save his people from their sins" (Matthew 1:21). Jesus did just that through His life and His death on the cross. This is atonement.

But what was the cause or reason for atonement? Why was it even necessary? What was the nature of Jesus' atonement? What is the result?

Jesus paid the penalty for our sins, and His perfect life now counts as ours! Jesus' righteousness is imputed to us.

"But why did Jesus have to die?"

Summary

The cause of the atonement

The *love and the justice* of God are the cause of atonement—the reasons it was necessary. It is not just love, because if this were the case, Jesus would not have had to die. Jesus had to pay the penalty that was due for sin.

Romans 3:24–25 says that Christ Jesus was "put forward as a propitiation by his blood, to be received by faith." A propitiation is a sacrifice that bears the wrath of God and turns God's wrath to favor.

God could not just welcome us back into relationship without someone taking a punishment as this would violate His holiness. In addition, we learn that God had stored up the punishment of those who sinned in the Old Testament to place on His Son (Romans 3:25; Hebrews 10:1–18).

The cause of the atonement was the love and the justice of God. God has paid for our sins, so we do not have to exist eternally in hell!

Questions

God sent His Son to die. What does this say about God's character? Is He a cruel God or a caring God? Why is that?

How does Jesus' death show both God's love and His justice?

Describe your experience of Christ's atonement.

The necessity of the atonement

It was not necessary for God to save anyone. He did not save the angels who rebelled. However, in His love, He chose to save some people. It says in Hebrews 10:4, "For it is impossible for the blood of bulls and goats to take away sins." Only the sacrifice of Christ could do it.

Even Jesus, in the Garden of Gethsemane, asked God if there was another way for us to be saved. But there was no other way (Luke 22:42). The only way for our sins to be forgiven was for someone who was perfect and sinless to pay the price.

Questions

Luke 24:26 says, "Was it not necessary that the Christ should suffer these things and enter into his glory?" Why do you think God chose to save some human beings?

How is Jesus' atonement different from the sacrifices of animals in the Old Testament?

How have you tried to atone for your own sins apart from Christ?

The nature of atonement

Had Jesus only offered Himself as a sacrifice and earned our forgiveness, this would be partial salvation. Our guilt would have been removed, and we would have been back to 'neutral' just like Adam before the fall. But then we would sin again.

Instead, Jesus came as a second Adam living in obedience to God for 33 years of His life so many would be made righteous through faith in Him.

Throughout Jesus' life, more and more responsibilities were put on Him, yet He never sinned. On the cross, He suffered incredible pain, more than just physical pain:

- Physical pain (beating, flogging, crucifixion)
- The pain of bearing the weight of our sin
- The agony of abandonment
- Pain of bearing the wrath of God

Jesus' horrible death shows us the destructiveness of sin and illustrates that sin is not trivial. Even though He hated sin to the depth of His being, He took on all the sin of those who would someday be saved. On the cross, Jesus was very much alone and separate from the disciples, and more importantly, from God the Father.

When Jesus called out, "It is finished" (John 19:30), the payment for sin was complete. This is the heart of atonement—that the justice of God was satisfied forever. When Jesus died, something happened between the Father and the Son. God put His wrath on Jesus; Jesus took the wrath and finally God's justice was satisfied. History was changed forever.

Questions

In what ways did Jesus' death do more than just remove our sin?

When God created the universe, He knew that His Son would die for mankind. What does this say about God?

Christians won't pay the penalty for their sins. Discuss the difficulties of living according to something that seems too good to be true.

The results of the atonement

Jesus lived a perfect, sinless life that is now credited to believer's lives. As it was predicted in the Old Testament, He died a sinner's death to pay the penalty we deserved. This overcame man's separation from God that was caused by sin.

God, through sending His Son to die, "has delivered us from the domain of darkness and transferred us to the kingdom of his beloved Son" (Colossians 1:13). We stand before God as recipients of what Jesus Christ did for us, and there is "no condemnation for those who are in Christ Jesus" (Romans 8:1).

Jesus endured the cross so we can enjoy the unimaginable blessings of heaven for all eternity.

Questions

Can you explain, in your own words, what the atonement is and what it means?

How does your experience of atonement affect your relationships?

If you will never pay for your sins, why not continue to sin?

Going Deeper

Know it:

➥ Watch the Q&A and discuss.

➥ In recent times, atonement has been under attack from within the church. How would you answer someone who related the atonement to 'cosmic child abuse'? (Isaiah 53:10).

Do it:

➥ How has Satan tried to undermine the atonement in your own life? Consider the following areas:

1. Feelings of condemnation
2. Times when you have judged another Christian and forgotten that Christ has paid for that person's sin

➥ Make a list of the sins you have committed that have troubled you the most. If you have trusted in Christ for forgiveness, write across the list "atoned for" and dispose of it.

Teach it:

→ Compose an email summarizing each aspect in this session. Include its impact on your own life. Email it to someone you know.

→ Invite a new believer to have coffee and explain the atonement to them.

What is the resurrection?

Introduction

Jesus did not remain dead. On the third day, He rose from the dead in triumph and victory!

All four of the Gospels have many details of what happened after Jesus rose again, what He did for the 40 days on earth and what happened as He went up into heaven.

In this session we will learn about the details of the resurrection, what the results of the resurrection are and the importance of Jesus' ascension into heaven.

Summary

Details of the resurrection

The Bible has many details of the
resurrection and what Jesus did after He
rose from the dead. His resurrection was
different from that of Lazarus and others
who were raised miraculously, because
Lazarus continued to age and eventually

died again, whereas Jesus had a body that would never grow weak,
get ill, age or die.

When Jesus rose, though He was immortal, He had a physical
body that the disciples could touch. He could also eat.

It is said in the Bible that our resurrected bodies will be like Jesus'
resurrected body. But what is that like?

1 Corinthians 15:42–44 says:

> "What is sown is perishable; what is raised is imperishable. It is sown in dishonor; it is raised in glory. It is sown in weakness; it is raised in power. It is sown a natural body; it is raised a spiritual body."

In eternity we will no longer grow old and may have a physical appearance of a 25 year old—someone in perfect physical condition. We will be far more beautiful (or handsome!) than today, with a glorious, personal, God-given radiance! We will have the strength to do all we need to glorify God, but will not be 'superhuman'. We will also be responsive to the work of the Holy Spirit.

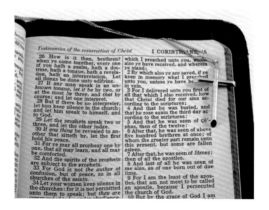

Questions

Jesus made sure that we know He rose with a physical body. Why do you think this is so important?

How will our resurrected body be better than the one we have today?

In what ways does our future resurrection give us hope today?

The results of the resurrection

All who trust in Christ have been, "born again to a living hope through the resurrection of Jesus Christ from the dead" (1 Peter 1:3). So one result of Christ's resurrection is that we are born again, or regenerated.

Though we do not get our new physical body yet, we get our renewed spirit, and this gives us the ability to live our lives in obedience to God.

Romans 6:14 says, "For sin will have no dominion over you, since you are not under law but under grace." This does not mean we are now perfect! It just means that the ruling power of sin over our lives is now broken.

Here are two out-workings of the resurrection:

- We will never be perfect in this life, but we should still strive for holiness with a strong hope of making progress.

- We should never stop growing in the Christian life.

Because we are united with Christ, His resurrection determines regeneration for all who believe and ensures justification before God. Christ's resurrection also guarantees our own future bodily resurrection.

There is an ethical significance to the resurrection as well—our work has eternal results. For example, if we share our knowledge of the Gospel and bring others to Christ, they too will be resurrected and will live with God and us forever.

Questions

What would you now say when asked why the resurrection is important?

Does it matter at what age we learn to trust in Christ? What difference can age make?

How do you think the results of the resurrection show in people's lives today?

Jesus' ascension into heaven

Forty days after Jesus' resurrection, He led His followers outside Jerusalem. Luke 24:50–51 says as Jesus was "lifting up his hands, he blessed them. While he blessed them, he parted from them and was carried up into heaven."

Acts 1:9–11 goes on to say that Jesus went into a cloud and was hidden from sight. The angels said He would return in the same way. Jesus was then exalted to the right hand of God and was given glory and honor that He did not have when He was a man.

Jesus has gone to prepare an eternal dwelling place for all of us who know our Redeemer lives, and He will come again to take us home (John 14:2–3).

So, the resurrection was not just a 'bringing back to life' but a pattern to show us that we too will be raised up in a renewed physical body, a body better than it was before.

Questions

Why does the resurrection of Christ matter to you?

Jesus has gone to prepare a place in heaven for us. What does this mean to you?

How does the resurrection add purpose to your everyday life?

Going Deeper

Know it:

→ Watch the Q&A and discuss.

→ Read 1 Corinthians 15 and summarize the main points with a bulleted list.

Do it:

→ Think about aging, disease and death in terms of yourself and those you know. Consider the difference the impact Christ's resurrection can have on those imperfections.

Teach it:

→ Telephone or speak in person to the people you thought about above and explain to them the hope you have because of the resurrection.

12 What is election (or predestination)?

Introduction

Some were chosen to be saved before the universe was even created; others will be passed over.

The doctrine of predestination, or election, is a controversial one in the church, but the Bible is clear about its existence. We see that some have been written into the Book of Life from before the foundation of the world (Revelation 17:8; 21:27). This is a great comfort to those who are saved.

Like all controversial doctrines, election raises many questions and objections in believers and non-believers alike. Are we really free? Is God really fair? Doesn't the Bible teach that God wants all people to be saved?

Only by looking in depth at the doctrine of election can we begin to understand what God's plan is for us.

Summary

Overview of the New Testament on election

Election is an "act of God before creation, in which He chooses some people to be saved, not on account of any foreseen merit in them, but only because of His sovereign good pleasure."

There are several places in the Bible which mention that God chose who would be saved before He made the universe. Acts 13:48 says, "When the Gentiles heard this, they began rejoicing and glorifying the word of the Lord, and as many as were appointed to eternal life believed."

Ephesians 1:4–6 says that God "chose us in him before the foundation of the world, that we should be holy and blameless before him."

Revelation 17:8 says that "the dwellers on earth whose names have not been written in the book of life from the foundation of the world will marvel to see the beast."

It is important to note that the Bible does not say that God chose everyone in Christ; He only chose those who would believe.

We must also note that the Bible does not say that we become elect once we believe in Christ, but that God chose us before He made the world (Ephesians 1:4).

Questions

The Bible says that not everyone is chosen to be saved. Does this help to explain why the world is like it is today? Why?

Acts 13:46–48 tells of Paul and Barnabas evangelizing the Gentiles. What does it tells us of the doctrine of election?

Read Romans 8:26–39. For what purpose does God tell us about election in these verses? Is this how we should use the doctrine of election?

12. What is election (or predestination)?

The application of election to our lives

The New Testament writers present the doctrine of election as a comfort to those who believe in Jesus.

Romans 8:29 says, "For those whom he foreknew he also predestined to be conformed to the image of his Son."

Paul is saying that if you look as far back into history as you can, God was working for your good. If you look at your recent past, God has been working for your good. If you look to the future when Christ will return, God will be working for your good.

People may use this doctrine to say, "God has chosen only certain people, therefore evangelism is pointless." Though it is true that God has only chosen certain people, He predestined a series of events which lead up to someone believing and this may include us sharing the Gospel with them.

We, like Paul, should share the Gospel because God has chosen some to be saved; we just do not know who. Evangelism is God's chosen vehicle to call the elect to Himself.

Questions

What does God want you to do in your neighborhood? Is it enough to mention the Gospel to people just once?

Should we ever 'give up' on somebody?

What would be the wrong way to use election?

What election does not mean

Election does not mean that our choices don't matter and that our actions don't have any consequences. This is fatalism. Our choices are actually extremely important, and Romans 10 teaches us that we have a responsibility to actively chose to believe in Jesus Christ by faith.

We should not think of an inflexible universe controlled by a machine. The Bible presents us as real people with real choices. Determinism does not take into account that God is a person who takes account of what we ask and do.

It does not mean that God's choice of us was based on His foreknowing that we would have faith. Scripture never speaks of our faith as the reason for God choosing us. He predestined us according to His will.

Questions

Do you think your choices matter, or do you subscribe to fatalism?

Do you think of the universe as inflexible and controlled by a machine—deterministic? Does God take account of what we ask and do?

How should we respond to the mystery of election?

Objections to the conclusions of election

"Are we really free?" People have many ideas as to what free actually means. Some think it means that God did not have anything to do with our choice, but the Bible does not say this. If we choose to respond to Christ in a positive or negative way, then we have made a real choice. This choice was in some way ordained before the foundation of the universe, and is therefore not a contradiction, but a mystery.

"If God chose some but not others, how can He be fair?" We must remember that God did not have to save anyone, yet He chose to save "a great multitude that no one could number, from every nation, from all tribes and peoples and languages" (Revelation 7:9).

12. What is election (or predestination)?

"Doesn't it say in the Bible that God wants everybody to be saved?" God has two wills, His revealed will and His secret will. His revealed will is that everyone should be saved, but His secret will is that not all will be saved. This is similar to God saying, "Do not murder," and yet He predestined that some would crucify Jesus.

The doctrine of election implies that there are some who will not be saved. Though it is a comfort for those who are saved, it may make us sad for those who will not be saved. However, the punishment of sinners will be righteous and in God's will. Election is a mystery which humbles us and causes us to give thanks to God. "For those who love God all things work together for good, for those who are called according to his purpose" (Romans 8:28).

Questions

What does 'free' mean to you, in the context of election? Did you chose to love Jesus?

Is God fair? Doesn't God want everyone to be saved? Should we tell others about Jesus, or is there no need to do this? What about evangelism?

How do you think God feels about those who are not saved?

Going Deeper

Know it:

→ Watch the Q&A and discuss.

→ A common teaching today is that God chooses those He knows (foreknows) will choose Him. Using a concordance, look up every reference in the New Testament to 'foreknow, foreknew, foreknowledge'. Look carefully at the context and see if such an interpretation is likely.

Do it:

→ Look at the main passages that teach election and notice the pastoral purpose of the passages. Practice applying these purposes to your own life.

Teach it:

→ This week explain to someone the pastoral benefits of the doctrine of election.

13 What does it mean to become a Christian?

Introduction

Becoming a Christian has much to do with things that happen in the spiritual realm and in our hearts. It is a lot more than just going to church, and you can't just join up like you do to a political party.

The Bible tells us that there is a specific order to what happens when someone becomes a Christian. God predestines believers to be saved; that person is then called; they decide to trust in Jesus by faith, then they are justified and will eternally be glorified (Romans 8:30).

Packed with information as to how we should call others to trust in Jesus, this hard-hitting session directly asks the question, "Are you saved?"

Summary

Effective calling

An effective call to trust in Jesus is a calling from God which demands and guarantees a response from the person who is called. This calling happens when God the Father speaks through the proclamations of a human being.

This call will bring results because, as the Bible says, becoming a Christian will lead you from darkness and alienation to the light, to fellowship with God in a new kingdom, with freedom and liberty, holiness and eternal life (1 John 1:5–7).

God speaks through us so that other people's hearts are changed.

Questions

Do you think God can work through any Christian to give an effective calling, or is it just those gifted in evangelism? Why is that?

God is able to call directly if He chooses to, but He actually uses other people to do the calling. What does this amazing responsibility mean to you?

God guarantees a positive response from those He effectually calls. How does this encourage us in evangelism?

General calling

Jesus said, "Come to me, all who labor and are heavy laden, and I will give you rest" (Matthew 11:28). A general calling happens when an evangelist, such as Billy Graham, calls many people. Yet only some will believe.

Therefore, a general calling is different from an effective calling, because in the general calling not all will respond positively.

Questions

If no one responds to a general calling, does this mean God was not present in the calling?

Why do you think some do not respond to a general calling?

Why should we tell everyone the Gospel if not all will respond?

The elements of a Gospel call

There are *three* elements to a Gospel call—explanation, invitation and a promise.

The explanation is the core facts of the Gospel, which are:

- We have all sinned and fall short of the glory of God.
- The penalty of sin is death.
- Jesus has paid this penalty for all who believe in Him.

The invitation is for the person to believe the Good News personally. Will you trust in Him? Will you commit your life to Him?

The promise is simple—if you trust in Jesus with your life, your sins will be forgiven and you will receive eternal life in Him.

Questions

Without looking back at the summary, can you name the three elements of a Gospel call?

Is there any value in explaining the facts of the Gospel to unbelievers if there is no invitation or promise stated afterwards? Why is that?

Share your own experience of the Gospel call.

13. What does it mean to become a Christian?

Regeneration

Once the call has been heard by an unbeliever who is going to come to faith, God does something in his or her heart.

Ezekiel 36:26 says, "And I will give you a new heart, and a new spirit I will put within you. And I will remove the heart of stone from your flesh and give you a heart of flesh."

The person will repent of his sin and trust in Christ. He will then be a completely new person or "a new creation" (2 Corinthians 5:17). He will have a desire to obey God's commands, and he will benefit from the work of the Spirit which produces joy, love and peace in a person's life.

Questions

How has your understanding changed as to why some do not 'get' the Gospel?

What are your thoughts on Christians who seem to be constantly unhappy and unsatisfied by life? How should we help them to find God's joy?

When did you first notice the fruits of regeneration in your own life? What were they?

Repentance and Faith

Conversion covers both repentance and faith in Jesus.

Becoming a Christian means that we must turn from sin. This is repentance. We must also then depend on Jesus Christ. This is faith. It is not possible to do one without the other.

Repentance and faith are like wings on a bird; both wings need to operate for the bird to fly.

13. What does it mean to become a Christian?

You do not have to 'become better' before becoming a Christian, and you do not have to live a moral life first. You must simply ask Jesus to forgive you, trust in Him and His work on the cross, and consciously decide to turn away from sin. At the point of conversion, we should confess specific sins to God.

However, there is more. We should use the initial repentance and faith as a pattern because we will sin again. Jesus taught us to pray "forgive us our debts" (Matthew 6:12) every day. After conversion, when we are Christians, we should live and walk by faith. We are not to begin with faith and later depend on ourselves.

Questions

What are your thoughts about those who say, "I am a Christian," yet have no outward signs that anything has changed?

Do you trust in Jesus as your Savior? Would you like to confess your sins now and receive the promise of eternal life?

If you already trust in Jesus, are there sins that you should confess so you can receive the joy of the Spirit into your life again right now?

Going Deeper

Know it:

- ➥ Watch the Q&A and discuss.
- ➥ Why is it necessary that regeneration precedes faith in logical sequence?

Do it:

- ➥ Make a list of the evidence of regeneration in your own life. Celebrate this in a prayer of thanksgiving to God.

Teach it:

- ➥ Share the Gospel this week with at least one person who is not a Christian.
- ➥ Teach a young Christian from the book of 1 John how to spot the evidence of regeneration in his or her life.

What are justification and adoption?

Introduction

After we become Christians, God has an array of wonderful blessings in store for us. Through the legal declaration of God in justification, we are declared righteous before Him.

In this session we will learn that ever since the teachings of Martin Luther and John Calvin, the Protestant church has re-discovered that justification is gained by faith alone, not through ongoing works.

Justification means that God declares us to be not guilty after forgiving all of our sins and seeing Christ's righteousness as 'imputed' or belonging to us.

As a separate but related issue, God also adopts us into His family when we believe in Jesus' name. We can then depend on Him to provide our needs because we are His children.

Summary

Justification is a legal declaration by God

Justification "is an instantaneous legal act of God in which He thinks of our sins as forgiven and thinks of Christ's righteousness as belonging to us, declaring us to be 'just' or morally righteous in His sight." We become righteous in the eyes of God because of the righteousness of Jesus. It is a declaration that we are righteous before God.

Just as regeneration is an act of God within us, justification is an external act of God about us.

Another expression that is often used is that God has imputed Jesus' righteousness to us, that He thinks of Christ's righteousness as belonging to us.

Paul, in Romans 5:1, is clear that justification comes after we respond to the Gospel call in Christ. It says simply that, "we have been justified by faith."

Questions

Justification means God thinks of us as forgiven and righteous forever. How does this provide stability and a firm foundation for our lives?

Is it fair that even though we continue to sin, God still accepts our sins as forgiven? Why?

Given election, effectual calling, regeneration and justification, is there any circumstance where God would reverse our justification?

Justification is a declaration that we are righteous before God

The historic view of the church is that justification happens at the time we trust in Jesus. It is a declaration of God that our sins are totally forgiven.

A recent and alternative view on justification is the 'New Perspective' teaching. This view implies that justification is a declaration that we are a part of the community of God. Final judgment will be based on our own 'works'—that is, on the entirety of the life we lived. We must note that the 'New Perspective' is at odds with Biblical truth and the historic position of the church.

Questions

Do you think justification happens at the time we trust in Jesus? What affect does this have on our thoughts about death?

There are many who believe in a delayed justification. Does this matter to you? Why?

Working in pairs, explain what justification is in your own words.

How do we gain justification?

Ephesians 2:8–9 says, "For by grace you have been saved through faith. And this is not your own doing; it is the gift from God, not a result of works, so that no one may boast."

Justification is gained by faith alone, but our faith does not have any merit on its own. Faith is actually the opposite of depending on ourselves. If justification came through love, joy, peace or kindness then we could choose to do these things; but faith is saying, "Lord Jesus, I can't save myself. I give up and I trust in You."

Roman Catholics would say that justification is gained through faith plus the sacraments, attending mass, penance, and the Eucharist (the Lord's Supper). Luther said that it is gained through faith alone, at the time we believe. True faith results in good works, proving salvation is genuine. Works don't gain salvation; they prove it to be true.

The application to our lives today is that even though as Christians we have memory of past sins and continue to sin each day, we will never be eternally condemned for those sins. God will never punish us and there is no penalty. God may discipline us to do us good, but He will not punish us—He just wants us to grow in holiness when we are in Christ.

We must look to God through Christ to freely give us what we cannot gain for ourselves.

14. What are justification and adoption?

Questions

When we believe in Jesus, we are instantly, and forever justified. Does this mean that we can live sinfully after this?

Christians do not believe in justification through 'works', so why should we continue to work for God once we are justified?

How does justification affect our joy and peace?

The gift of adoption

In John 1:12 we are told, "to all who did receive him, who believed in his name, he gave the right to become children of God."

Adoption is separate from justification. It means that we become members of God's family. We are also told in Ephesians 2:2–3 that those who don't believe in Christ are "sons of disobedience" and "children of wrath."

We can become like partners in the family business. God is not distant and we are not like slaves in the modern sense, but we actually become the children of God. By having this privilege, we can ask God for help. There is also a future aspect to this adoption—one day we will receive renewed bodies as sons and daughters of God.

There is one more aspect of adoption which is not so pleasant—that of suffering. God allows us to go through suffering in part because at these times we have a special closeness to Him.

We follow the path that Jesus followed. We must remember that "the sufferings of this present time are not worth comparing with the glory that is to be revealed to us" (Romans 8:18).

When Christ returns, our tears will be wiped away and we will dwell forever in the fullness of the kingdom of our Father.

Christian Beliefs Study Guide

Questions

What does being a child of God mean to you?

How does believing that we are adopted and loved by God affect our relationships with ourselves, with other people and with God?

Why does God allow us to suffer? How can our knowledge of our adoption by God help us through the tough times?

Going Deeper

Know it:

- → Watch the Q&A and discuss.
- → Compare Biblical justification to the 'New Perspective on Paul'.

Do it:

- → What would have been different for you in the last couple of weeks had you been fully believing the truth about your justification and adoption?

Teach it:

- → Without justification there is no Gospel and no church.
- → Write a summary of justification and email it to someone you know.
- → Telephone at least three people this week and tell them about justification.

15 What are sanctification and perseverance?

Introduction

There is more to Christian life than simply starting in the Christian way and giving your life to Christ. Once we are justified, we cannot simply sit back and do nothing else.

In this session we will learn that sanctification is a progressive work of God and man that makes us more and more free from sin and like Christ in our lives. This work ends for our spirits when we are made perfect at death and for our bodies when Christ returns. There is a God-ordained tension in sanctification between God's sovereign work and our human responsibility to respond and obey by faith.

The second part of the session deals with perseverance and how we must continue in the Christian life to the end. Many will wonder if they are true believers. In this part of the session, we will learn many ways to have great assurance that we are saved.

Summary

Sanctification

Sanctification is a progressive work which involves both God and man. It makes us increasingly free from sin and more like Christ. We should expect to make progress in our sanctification, but we will never achieve perfection until Christ returns.

Immediately, at the point of conversion, we are no longer slaves to sin. Even though this is a significant step toward sanctification, we will still sin. Therefore, we should pray daily to grow in sanctification throughout our lives. When we die, our own spiritual sanctification is completed, for our bodies stay in the grave and our souls go to God. Full sanctification happens when Christ returns and we have our resurrection bodies.

God gives us the power to be sanctified through the Holy Spirit, giving us an ability to grow and be responsive to the Scriptures and God's guidance. We must strive for holiness and God will honor our efforts. If we do not strive, we can become lazy Christians. On the other hand, if we neglect the fact that God has a role in our sanctification, we will become both frustrated and proud.

Some motives for obedience to God in the Christian life are the desire to:

- please God
- keep a clear conscience before God
- be a vessel for noble use
- see unbelievers come to Christ by observing our lives
- receive God's blessing on our lives and ministries
- avoid God's displeasure and discipline
- see greater heavenly reward
- experience a deeper walk with God
- know that angels will glorify God for our obedience.
- have peace and joy in our lives
- do what God commands because His commands are right.

15. What are sanctification and perseverance?

Questions

What can we do to strive for holiness?

What is your greatest motivation for sanctification?

In which ways do you think God will honor our commitment and energy?

Think of Christians you respect. Do you see a progressive sanctification throughout their lives?

Perseverance

We are told that all who are born again will persevere, meaning they will be kept by God until the end and will continue in the Christian faith. Several verses in the Bible tell us that once God has begun a work in us, He will continue the work until the coming of Jesus Christ (Philippians 1:6, John 6:38–40, 1 Thessalonians 5:23–24).

There are also several verses that tell us only those who persevere are truly born again (Hebrews 3:14, Colossians 1:23, 1 John 2:19). These verses serve as a warning that there will be some who come and are part of the fellowship of the church for a while, but who exhibit no real change in their lives, proving they had no real faith. Christian works are not a condition but a consequence of true salvation.

This may lead us to wonder whether we are true believers. As we grow in the Christian life, we gain a greater and greater assurance, but it is helpful to ask ourselves two main questions:

- Do I have a present trust in Christ and His ongoing work in my life?

- If I died tonight and God asked me, "Why should I let you into heaven?" what would I say?

If our answer is that we have been a good person, there is no assurance that we are a believer. However, if our genuine answer is that we trust in Christ, we have greater indication that we really are a Christian.

Other helpful questions are:

- Do you sense a testimony of the Holy Spirit in your heart?

- Do you desire to pray for others?

- Do you see the fruit of the Spirit (in general) in your life?

- Do you see fruitfulness in having some impact on others?

- Do you have a sense of a continuing present relationship with Christ?

- Is there an acceptance of the sound teachings of the church?

- Do you have a love for other Christians?

- Do you continue in Christian fellowship?

- Do you have a willingness to give to a brother in need?

- Can you see a pattern in your life of growing obedience to God?

Questions

Only those who persevere are born again, and only those who are born again will persevere. What are your thoughts on this?

If you died tonight, what would you say to God about your life and why He should let you into heaven?

Do you think that perseverance and sanctification work together to help you grow more holy? Why?

Going Deeper

Know it:

→ Watch the Q&A and discuss.

→ In his letters, Paul often spends the first half telling us about grace before exhorting us to holiness. Why is that?

→ A popular teaching is that Christians can lose their salvation. How would you respond to this based on Scripture?

Do it:

→ Reflect on the list of motives for obedience. Bring any unhelpful or inappropriate motives you may have had to the Lord in prayer and ask Him to help you change them.

Teach it:

→ This week, explain to another Christian the priority and process of growing in holiness.

16 What is death?

Introduction

Death is not a punishment for Christians. Rather, it is the completion of one part of our sanctification in that our spirits are cleansed from their sin. Although death in itself is not good and was brought about by sin through the fall,  God will bring good in the death of Christians.

As Christians, our bodies rest in the grave when we die, but our spirits are raised up to be in God's presence. When Jesus returns, our souls will be joined with our resurrection bodies and we will live forever.

The outlook is not so good for non-believers. When they die, their souls go to eternal punishment and their bodies remain in the grave. At the time of Christ's coming, they too will be raised up and will stand before God in final judgment.

This session deals with the important things that happen when we die, what we should think about death and the attitude we should have towards it.

Summary

Why do Christians die?

At the point of death, there is a completion of one part of our sanctification. Our spirits are completely cleansed from sin. It is not until Christ returns that we get our resurrection body, when our body and soul will be joined together and made perfect forever.

God decided that it would be best for Christians not to experience all of the blessings of salvation at once, just as parents do not give their children everything they want all at once.

We can die because we still live in a world under the effects of the fall. Even though we are regenerated and renewed, we still live in a world marked by sin; not all of our lives are made right and death has not been removed.

In God's eyes, preserving our lives and our comfort is not the highest priority; the first priority is obedience to Him for His glory.

Although we do not think of death as something good and it is not good in itself, God does bring good from it. It is contrary to the way God created us. However, God works out all things in accordance with the counsel of His will (Ephesians 1:11), even death! It was brought in through sin (Romans 5:12), but because of Christ, it has no ultimate victory over all who believe (1 Corinthians 15:54–55).

Our goal is to glorify God and to enjoy Him fully forever!

Questions

How do you think the teaching from Revelation 2:10, "Be faithful unto death, and I will give you the crown of life," is a comfort?

What are your thoughts about death? Is death something to look forward to or to fear?

Is death still a taboo subject today? Why?

What happens when Christians die?

We should not view our own death with fear. Hebrews 2:15 says that Jesus died to "deliver all those who through fear of death were subject to lifelong slavery." This lack of fear can be an amazing testimony to non-Christians.

When we die, our souls immediately go into God's presence. Our body remains in the ground and is buried.

There is no need to pray for those believers who die because they are somewhere far better than on earth. Instead, we should pray for the comfort of those who remain. It is, however, not wrong to be sad when someone dies. Even Jesus wept when He reached the tomb of Lazarus. But this grief is not a bitter grief; it is mixed with joy and is a time when we can draw close to God.

Questions

Do you fear death? What should we do if we have this fear?

Should we be sad when someone dies, or should we rejoice? What does modern culture say about how we behave at this time?

What do you think about scientific attempts to extend life indefinitely?

What happens when unbelievers die?

When people who have rejected Christ die, their souls immediately go to eternal punishment but their bodies remain in the ground until Christ returns. At that time, both believers and unbelievers will be raised and will stand before God at the final judgment.

The Bible never says that people will have a second chance to trust in Christ after death. We "die once, and after that comes judgment" (Hebrews 9:27).

However, we often do not have absolute certainty that a friend or loved one has continued to reject Christ to the end. We simply do not know their hearts. If we are asked whether we think an unbeliever has gone to heaven, we should speak with thankfulness about their lives and good qualities and say we can trust the goodness and justice of God, but we should not speak falsely. This will often be a good time for saying that Jesus promises "everyone who lives and believes in me shall never die" (John 11:26).

Questions

The Bible indicates that there is no chance of salvation for unbelievers after death. What do you think about this?

Are you afraid of standing before God? What can we do to feel more confident about this?

Think of people you know you need to share the Gospel with. What is your plan?

When are Christians raised from the dead?

When believers die, their bodies remain in the ground, but their souls go immediately into the presence of God. Then we wait for the redemption of our bodies.

Glorification does not happen immediately when we die. Instead, we wait until the day Christ returns. On that day, all the bodies of all believers from all of history will be raised from the dead and made new.

If we have not died when Jesus returns, our bodies will be changed at the moment He returns.

Although death itself is an enemy, God has good purposes for us in death and will bring good to us through the process. When believers die, they go immediately into the presence of God; but when unbelievers die, they go immediately to a place of judgment with separation from God. On the day Christ returns, all will be raised for resurrection of life or resurrection of judgment.

Questions

What good can come from death? Why is it an enemy?

How would you talk about this to an unbelieving friend with a life-threatening illness?

How do you feel about all people having a physical body for eternity?

Going Deeper

Know it:

- ➥ Watch the Q&A and discuss.

- ➥ Some people teach that there is no conscious state between death and resurrection. How would you respond to this teaching based on Scripture?

Do it:

- ➥ Write a newspaper article reporting your own death and the impact your life had on others. Write the article based on what you would like that impact to be. What life adjustments do you need to make?

Teach it:

- ➥ Write a brief summary of death and a Biblical response to the idea of "soul sleep."

17 What is the church?

Introduction

We are called to Christ individually and Christ calls us together corporately into the community of the Church. John Wesley said, "The Bible knows nothing of solitary religion." In this session, we will learn that the church is both visible and invisible, with local and universal expressions.

There are many metaphors for the church, and each one can be helpful when we think about our relationships with each other and with God.

We will also learn several key pointers that let us know what a church is and how pure a church is. Finally, we will see the three purposes of the church.

"So, what is the church?"

Summary

The church is visible and invisible

Ephesians 5:25 says "Christ loved the church and gave himself up for her."

The church is, by definition, the community of all believers for all time. The church consists of all the men and women who have been believers, the believers who are alive now and those in the future who will be true believers in Jesus. It will not be complete until the last person is saved.

Some say the church did not begin until the day of Pentecost, but this would mean that John the Baptist, Moses and Abraham would be excluded from the church.

We cannot see the spiritual condition of people's hearts. We don't truly know if they are believers or not. There will be people in your neighborhood who are believers, but you may not know enough about them to know this. 2 Timothy 2:19 says, "The Lord knows those who are his."

The invisible church is the church *as God sees it.* In the invisible church, 100% of the members are true believers and 0% outside of it are true believers. The visible church is the church *as Christians on earth see it.* Less than 100% are true believers and there may be many non church-goers, who are not visible believers, but who are part of the invisible church. You may be surprised at those who are not in the visible church and those who are when the Lord returns. It is good to exercise a benevolent evaluation of people you meet.

Questions

Only the Lord knows those who are His. How can we have any idea if someone is a part of the true church?

How can we ensure that we have a benevolent evaluation when we meet people?

When did the church begin and why?

Metaphors for the church

In the New Testament, the word "church" is used to describe different groups of Christians from very small to very large. Some would say there should only be one church in a city, a city-wide church. But this is not true. There can be meetings in houses as well as many local churches in a large city.

We should also consider that there is a universal expression of "church" as a whole.

Some metaphors in the Bible for the church are:

- A family
- The bride of Christ
- A body
- The body of Christ
- A new temple
- A holy priesthood
- The vine and the branches
- An olive tree
- A field that bears crops

We should be willing to see the church from many perspectives, as each will teach us different things. We must not focus too much on any one metaphor since we could miss out on many other ideas.

Questions

Which of the metaphors is the one you hear mentioned the most? Why is that?

Which metaphor could be most helpful for you to grow in your Christian life right now?

Discuss the metaphors that are least familiar to you.

What makes a church a church?

Since the time of the Reformation, there has been a teaching that there are two things needed to make a proper church:

- Sound preaching of the Word.

- Correct administration of the sacraments.

The sacraments, in this case, mean baptism and the Lord's Supper. Baptism is the one thing that Jesus commanded us to do that marks becoming part of the community of God's people. We should, however, be concerned if a church baptizes everyone including believers and non-believers alike.

The Lord's Supper is a sign of a continuation of the fellowship of the church.

We should probably also add another mark of the church, because today there are many different types of church organizations which may not be churches in themselves. This extra mark is:

- Attempting to function as a church.

Questions

Can a church be a church if it does not have sound preaching of the Word? Why?

Can a church be a church if it does not correctly administer the sacraments? Why?

Can a church be a church if it is not attempting to function as a church? Why?

The purity and unity of the church

There are a number of false churches such as Jehovah's Witnesses, Muslims, Scientologists, Christian Scientists and Mormons. These "churches" often teach that you must earn your own salvation in some way.

Even among true churches, there are distinctions to be made with some being more pure and others less pure. We can tell how pure a church is by considering a number of questions.

- Does it have sound doctrine?
- Does it have good Bible teaching?
- Does it have good fellowship among members?
- Is there a devotion to prayer?
- Are members growing in holiness?
- Is there effective witness?

Jesus prayed that we all might be one, but this does not mean that there must be one worldwide church government. God wants us to strive for both the purity and the unity of the church.

Questions

Do you believe we must earn our own salvation? What are your thoughts about churches who teach this perspective?

What should our response be if we meet people from what we think to be a false church?

How can you help increase the purity of your church?

The purpose of the church

There are three tasks the church should carry out. It should:

- minister to God.

- minister to believers.

- minister to the world.

We should worship God and live to praise Him. Worship is, therefore, a major part of the fulfillment of the purpose of the church. It is not just a lead up to the sermon.

To the world, the church should preach the Gospel and show mercy, just as Jesus healed the sick and cared for the poor. We should love our neighbors as we love ourselves.

God gives each person a gift with which to minister to other Christians and build the church.

Questions

In what ways can you minister to God?

In what ways can you minister to believers?

In what ways can you minister to the world?

Going Deeper

Know it:

- ➥ Watch the Q&A and discuss.
- ➥ How do you evaluate whether your church should have fellowship with another church? Support your answer from Scripture.

Do it:

- ➥ Evaluate your contribution in ministry to building God's church. Do you need to make any changes?
- ➥ Examine your feelings about Christians who "do" church differently than you. Talk to the Lord about this.

Teach it:

- ➥ Explain to another Christian the three purposes of the church and help him or her to formulate a plan to grow in each area.

What will happen when Christ returns?

Introduction

Many passages in the Bible teach that Christ will return personally and bodily to the earth and that every eye will see Him.

This session deals with the signs that will be seen before Christ returns and whether we can expect Him to return today or sometime soon. There are several different understandings of what the Bible says, and we will learn about some ways the Scripture has been interpreted.

One thing we can agree on, though, is that Christ will visibly return and will reign in heaven and on earth for all time.

"Could Christ return today?"

Summary

Christ will return personally

The general term for the study of the end-times is eschatology, the study of the last things. We are told in many places in the Bible that Jesus will return bodily and visibly.

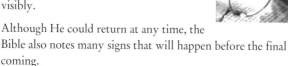

Although He could return at any time, the Bible also notes many signs that will happen before the final coming.

Mark 13:10 "And the Gospel must first be proclaimed to all nations."

Mark 13:22 "False christs and false prophets will arise and perform signs and wonders, to lead astray, if possible, the elect."

Mark 13:24–25 "But in those days, after that tribulation, the sun will be darkened, and the moon will not give its light, and the stars will be falling from heaven, and the powers in the heavens will be shaken."

2 Thessalonians 2:1–3 "Now concerning the coming of our Lord Jesus Christ ... that day will not come, unless the rebellion comes first, and the man of lawlessness is revealed."

Romans 11:26 "all Israel will be saved."

If there were only these verses in the Bible, we would not expect the return any time soon. But these verses are actually there to heighten our expectation. In actual fact, there are several verses that say Christ could come back any day "at an hour you do not expect" (Matthew 24:44; Matthew 25:13).

Questions

Should we spend our time trying to determine when Christ will return?

What do you think "all Israel will be saved" (Romans 11:26) means? Does this mean the Jews, or all the people of God?

How can we guard against being deceived?

Christ could come at any time

Some people claim that since the signs of Christ's return have not yet happened, it will take at least a generation before the end comes. Others hold the pre-tribulational view popularized by the *Left Behind* series of books. This view teaches that Christ will come secretly and take up all believers to Himself for seven years while there is a time of tribulation on the earth before He returns again.

1 John 4:3 says, "This is the spirit of the antichrist." Yet another view is that it is unlikely, but possible, that the signs have already been fulfilled. Although Western Christians enjoy a degree of freedom to practice their faith, many Christians living in Muslim countries could view the suffering and tribulation of their lives as a sign of the Great Tribulation (Revelation 7:14). It could also be pointed out that more Christian martyrs have died per year over the last few years than ever before in history.

There is some uncertainty. As humans, we are used to dealing with things that are unlikely, but possible. We have insurance policies, for example, and wear seat belts. We should prepare for Christ's coming even though we do not know when it will be.

Questions

Which view of the tribulation do you find most scriptural and why?

What are your thoughts about the number of martyrs being made at present in many countries? Is this a sign?

Do you eagerly hope for Christ's return?

Christ's return and the millennium

Revelation 20:1–6 raises a controversy because it mentions that Satan will be bound for "a thousand years." A millennium means one thousand years, but when does the thousand years start?

The **Amillennial View**—Revelation 20 refers to the present "church age" and the millennium is just a symbolic time for that period. At the end of this, Jesus will return and there will be the final judgment. This explanation is simple to understand.

The **Postmillennial View**—We are in the church age which is an age of increasing Gospel expansion and victory over the darkness. A millennium period will follow in which nations will be transformed by the Gospel. Christ will come at the end of that age for the final judgment. This is a very optimistic view which tends to become popular when there are large revivals in the church.

The **Premillennial View**—The millennium will come suddenly and Jesus will return to earth as it begins. Jesus will then reign on the earth for a thousand years (Revelation 20:4–5) and Satan and his demons will have no influence on earth during this time. The pre-tribulational pre-millennial position is a variation on this, holding that Jesus secretly comes back and takes believers to Himself for seven years. During these seven years comes the tribulation and the rebellion, then Jesus returns for the final judgment.

It must be said that the differences in these theories might not make a big difference in how we live the Christian life. As long as we insist on there being a visible, bodily return of Christ, any of the views can be helpful and contribute something to our understanding.

We can all agree that when Jesus does return, He will reign in heaven and on earth for all time.

Questions

Do you think it is important to try to understand Christ's return and what the millennium means? Why?

Which millennial view do you hold and why?

Why do you think the Bible is not as explicit about the timing of the second coming as we might like?

Going Deeper

Know it:

- ⇁ Watch the Q&A and discuss.
- ⇁ Examine the evidence for a pre-tribulational or a post-tribulational rapture.

Do it:

- ⇁ Has the topic of Christ's return been either too prominent and distracting you, or not prominent enough leaving your hope a little unfocused?

Teach it:

- ⇁ Write a clear summary of the main millennial views. Explain them to another believer along with which one you think to be most Scriptural and why.

What is the final judgment?

Introduction

There have been many lesser judgments that God has decreed over time, such as the destruction of Sodom and Gomorrah (Genesis 19:24) and the flood of Noah's day (Genesis 6–9). These are small forerunners of the day of final judgment.

Both believers and non-believers, along with all of the angels, will be judged. We will all stand before God to give account of ourselves. It will be a completely fair judgment.

In this session we will learn what will happen at the final judgment, why there needs to be a judgment, what we can learn from the judgment and how this applies to our lives. We will also learn some of what will happen to unbelievers.

Summary

What happens at the final judgment?

At the final judgment, there will be a day of wrath when God's righteous judgment will be revealed. Acts 17:31 says God "will judge the world in righteousness" through Jesus Christ. It will be a time for rewarding God's servants, and therefore should not strike terror into our hearts.

The Bible does not teach salvation through works, but it does teach that our works will be evaluated by God. God will be fair, determining reward or loss of reward by what we have done on earth with the capacities and gifts He gave us. We must, however, remember that there is no condemnation for those who trust in Jesus, and believers will not go to hell.

The Bible tells us in 1 Corinthians 3:12–15 that we should build on the foundation, Christ, with "gold, silver, precious stones" and not "wood, hay, straw" because our judgment will be "by fire." This means that we must be careful to do the Lord's work in His way for His glory. What we do on earth matters!

The judgment must be balanced with the fact that believers will be filled with joy in heaven. We may lose rewards (1 Corinthians 3:15), but our joy will be complete in heaven because our heavenly satisfaction will come from our delight in God. The Bible also seems to hint at differing levels of heavenly responsibilities (Luke 19:17).

Questions

Believers should not fear the final judgment. How hard should we work for God's glory? Will it matter when the judgment comes?

Romans 2:8 says, "for those who are self-seeking and do not obey the truth, but obey unrighteousness, there will be wrath and fury." What does this say to modern society?

Every deed, whether good or evil, will be judged. Do the little things matter? Why?

What is the purpose of the final judgment?

God already knows what is in our hearts, so the judgment is not for this reason. Judgment is so God's justice, mercy and wisdom can be displayed.

The judgment will be completely fair and we will acknowledge it as true. It will match our own built-in sense of justice at that time. Even the judgment of unbelievers will feel fair to us, as we will see their sin in its entirety.

Just as we can understand that Satan and the demons must be judged appropriately, unbelievers must be judged. We will see this as perfectly right and just.

Questions

Do you believe that we are able to earn rewards in heaven? Why? How should this affect the way we act today?

We should not be competitive to gain favor with God. How should we instead "stir up one another to love and good works" (Hebrews 10:24)?

What are your thoughts about judging angels?

The application of the final judgment

There are a number of useful applications for our knowledge of the final judgment.

- The final judgment assures us that the universe is fair.

- It satisfies our need for justice. God is in control and will bring a proper end to every situation. For example, we may have been mistreated, but we will receive the inheritance we are due from the Lord. This means we should not try to seek personal vengeance now (Romans 12:19).

- We should seek to treat others fairly and justly because we have a Master in heaven who will be eternally just and fair with us at the final judgment.

- We are able to forgive more easily knowing that all accounts will be settled either through the death of Christ or by punishment of the unbeliever himself. We should trust in Jesus for this.

- We should obey the Lord each day and lay up treasures in heaven.

We are taught that the civil authorities are the servants of God on earth and are, in some small way, a reflection of the final judgment. Therefore, we may seek justice for some wrong-doing from courts of law (Romans 13).

The final judgment should also encourage us to tell others about the good news of Jesus.

Questions

What is your natural reaction when someone wrongs you, even in a small way? What should it be? What does this tell us about how God must feel?

Are the civil authorities today acting as God's servants for justice on the earth? How should we respond to the laws in our own country?

Hell

At the final judgment, those who have rejected the claims of Jesus will go to hell, a place of eternal punishment. The passages in the Bible that teach us about hell can be disturbing (Matthew 5:22–30; Matthew 10:28; Mark 9:43–47).

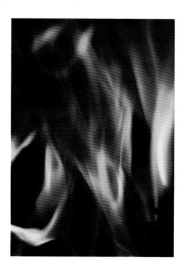

Some descriptions of hell are:

- Eternal fire
- Where their worm does not die and the fire is not quenched
- A place of torment
- A place with no rest, day or night

We should not fear hell if we trust in Christ. Our life is "hidden with Christ in God" (Colossians 3:3), and we will appear with Him in glory because of His righteousness counting for us!

However, even though God says, "I have no pleasure in the death of the wicked" (Ezekiel 33:11), evil will not go unpunished; God will always be just.

19. What is the final judgment?

Some, such as the Seventh Day Adventists, deny the doctrine of hell, and instead believe in annihilationism. This view states that there is no eternal punishment. Unbelievers will just cease to exist. Although this may sound appealing, it does not match the teaching in the Bible.

Both believers and unbelievers will be judged. The final judgment will be a time of rewards, great fairness and joy for believers, but a time of great sorrow for unbelievers.

Questions

What do you believe about hell?

Should we fear hell? Is this a motivation to trust more in Christ? Why?

How can we use our knowledge of hell to motivate us to evangelize more effectively?

Going Deeper

Know it:

→ Watch the Q&A and discuss.

→ How would you respond from Scripture to the annihilationist view?

Do it:

→ Spend time in prayer thanking God for salvation and praying for those you know who do not know Christ personally.

Teach it:

→ Share with someone who is not a Christian your story of avoiding hell and why hell is just and fair.

What is heaven?

Introduction

After the final judgment, those who believe in Jesus will begin the full enjoyment of the life they have longed for. We will live for eternity in the presence of God.

There will be a renewed heaven and a renewed earth for us to enjoy, free from sin. We will have work to do to fill our time and we will be able to enjoy all the fruits of the tree of life, while learning new skills and glorifying God.

Best of all, we will see the face of God. We will be able to worship and interact with Him as we dwell in His presence.

"But, where is heaven? What will it be like? What will we do there?"

Summary

The renewed heaven and earth

The Bible itself uses the word heaven, but more fully it uses the term "new heaven and new earth." The Bible promises that all creation will be renewed. Pain, suffering and sorrow will be removed. The Bible leads us to believe that the earth will be renewed, not recreated (Romans 8:21–22).

Although God is present everywhere, heaven is that place where God makes His presence especially known. Some say that heaven is not a physical place, and instead is just a state of mind. But the Bible teaches us that it is a real place, probably not too far from the earth, in our own space/time universe. No one knows where it is, but Jesus' body went somewhere when He was taken up to heaven at the ascension.

The Bible spends very little time referring to the stars—most references are to do with the earth. This is the focus of God's special activity.

The renewed earth will not have 'thorns and thistles', which means that there will not be any of the physical things which make our lives so painful. We will find out exactly what the Garden of Eden was like and will be able to enjoy it with our renewed bodies since the curse from Genesis will be removed!

Questions

Heaven is a physical place, not merely a state of mind. Discuss.

As children, it is simple to understand that heaven is the place where God is. Does this become harder to accept as we grow older?

What do you think heaven will be like?

What will we do In heaven?

Like Adam and Eve in the Garden of Eden, we will both work and play in heaven. The work will be both fulfilling and fun. We will also worship, have fellowship with friends, explore, learn and do many of the other things that we do today.

Revelation 19:9 says, "Blessed are those who are invited to the marriage supper of the Lamb." This will be the best food we could imagine. We will also be able to eat from the Tree of Life, which will have amazing and delicious fruits. There will no doubt be music, painting, arts, drama and theater. We will be able to learn all of the skills that we have always wanted to learn.

In our lives now, God has given us abilities and desires that echo what we will be able to do in heaven. We can rest assured that it won't be boring!

Questions

What skills do you want to learn in heaven? Would starting to learn them now help to glorify God?

We will work in heaven. What are your thoughts about this?

The glory of God

God's glory is undeniably evident in heaven. All will willingly cooperate with Him.

There will be no pain or sorrow because God and His glory are there. We will be able to interact and worship with Him as we were originally designed to do.

Revelation 21:23 says that in heaven "the city has no need of sun or moon to shine on it, for the glory of God gives it light, and its lamp is the Lamb." This was seen in the Bible when the shepherds saw a radiance in the sky when Jesus was born.

Our greatest joy will be when we see God's face and when we can dwell in His presence (Job 19:26; Revelation 22:4). It is definitely something to look forward to.

Questions

What do you think rewards in heaven will consist of?

How can heaven help us to persevere now?

What will you miss least about living in a sin-cursed world? What will be the corresponding joy in heaven for you?

Going Deeper

Know it:

- ↪ Watch the Q&A and discuss.

- ↪ Make a list of a number of New Testament references to heaven and its activities.

Do it:

- ↪ Apply the hope of heaven to the current difficulties in your life. What difference does this make?

Teach it:

- ↪ Telephone another Christian who is in difficult life circumstances. Encourage that person regarding the certainties and pleasures of heaven.

Resourcing with a mission

Clear Cut Media was established in the UK in 2006 by two pastors, Trevor Allin and Andrew Hutchinson. Wrestling with how to best help Christians grow in their faith, Trevor and Andrew searched for resources that would not just increase head knowledge but affect the heart and lifestyle. Some resources already existed and some needed to be created. It was with this vision that Clear Cut Media (CCM) was born.

After various projects they saw clearly the need for a foundational resource that would help bring stability and renewal to the church. A resource was needed that all Christians could access, no matter what their stage of faith. It would need to be comprehensive in teaching all the main doctrines of the Bible but in a way that led people to worship and change. Dr. Wayne Grudem was contacted because of his unique combination of expertise, passion, and love for the Lord.

With the *Christian Beliefs* DVD course being one of the most significant and high impact resources currently available, distribution centers have been established in the United Kingdom, United States, and Australia.

To help select and produce further resources that are relevant to helping Christians grow in their faith, we would be very interested in hearing about how you are using this course, together with any feedback you may have. Please do let us know by e-mailing feedback@clearcutmedia.tv.

For more information about Clear Cut Media please contact us at info@clearcutmedia.tv or visit www.clearcutmedia.tv/us.

 CLEARCUTMEDIA